MAURITIUS
Light and Space

Photographs
Christian Bossu-Picat

Text
Dan Callikan

The Star and Key of the Indian Ocean

Looking at the island through the porthole as his plane is about to land, the visitor is surprised by the sheer diversity of the scenery that immediately arrests his gaze : the dark blue waters of the high seas; the slender ring of protective coral reef upon which the waves keep breaking in a flurry of white foam; the protected lagoon with its translucent waters unveiling all the hues of blue and green in the clear luminosity of the tropical sun; the immaculate white sand beaches etching the frontier with the undulating dark green sugar cane fields; the gently rounded hills rising out of the plains; the dark sculpturesque mountains standing majestically against the sparkling blue sky and the clear horizon.

Watching this sublime scenery in its serene beauty, the visitor will hardly believe that such an island was born out of a tremendous volcanic eruption that tore the bowels of the Indian Ocean more than seven million years ago in an explosion of elemental violence.

As time passed by, the lava flows were covered with vegetation, a dense tropical forest gradually transformed the island into a paradise for numerous species of lizards, reptiles, tortoises and birds among which the most well-known, the dodo, has become a universal symbol for all species already extinct or threatened with extinction. All these creatures lived in peace and tranquillity in this Garden of Eden before the Fall.

It was in 1598 that the Dutch sailors first set foot in this idyllic scenery. These sailors formed part of an expedition led by admirals Van Nyck and Van Warwyck heading towards their possessions in the East Indies after having rounded the Cape of Good Hope. But fate had predicted another destination for them. Blown by the winds of a cyclone, they reached the shores of this virgin island.

Mauritius became engulfed in a fascinating history as from that time. The Dutch, the French and the British successively used Mauritius as a port of call or as a colony in their quests for exotic products. People also came from Africa, India and China and contributed to the creation of a human patchwork befitting this dream island. This engendered a rainbow nation destined to give birth to a new personality integrating the rich cultural ingredients coming from the four corners of the world in an ever evolving synthesis.

This book aims at portraying the convergence of the rich natural and human diversity, multiplied by the infinite interplay of light, shade and colour in this island bathed in a luminous atmosphere imparting a natural rhythm to human activity itself.

Let us allow ourselves to be permeated by the special atmosphere conveyed to us surreptitiously by the scenes filmed with passion by artist-photographer Christian Bossu-Picat in search of the essence in all things.

Before embarking on this quest, however, we shall make a brief survey of the economic, political and human history of Mauritius in order to get better acquainted with this population whose motto is "Unity in Diversity" – unity forged through time in the quest of a common destiny transcending racial, linguistic, religious and political differences.

Dan Callikan

Geography, History, Population, Economy

Location

Situated in the southwest of the Indian Ocean, just beneath the tropic of Capricorn, between 19°50 and 20°32 latitude south and 57°18 and 57°46 longitude east, Mauritius is a small island anchored 2000 kms away from the eastern African coastline and 800 kms east of Madagascar. The island, which is 65 kms long and 45 kms wide spans an area of 1860 square kilometres while its exclusive economic zone extends over an area of more than one and a half million square kilometres. The coastal plains gently rise towards a central plateau reaching 600 m above sea level while the highest mountain, the Piton de la Rivière Noire, in the west, peaks at 827 metres.

The island emerged out of the ocean seven and a half million years ago as a result of volcanic activity. The cataclysm that presided over its birth has endowed Mauritius with a varied and picturesque landscape: tempting white sand beaches stretching over endless kilometres, adventure-loaded mountain sceneries, inland valleys, steep river banks and patches of dark green endemic forest.

Summer stretches all the way from November to April enlivening the atmosphere with a giddy but ever-pleasant 27°C to 33°C, while what Mauritians call winter, which is in fact a milder summer, experiences amiable temperatures ranging from 15°C to 25°C. The transition between the two seasons is as natural and easy as dew returning to the mother clouds on an early sunny morning. Summer brings with it the cyclonic season though, and those cyclones that cross over the island from time to time bear testimony to the fierce and destructive forces of Nature. Elder Mauritians still remember with awe the damages caused by memorable cyclones that hit Mauritius in 1945, 1960, 1975 and 1994 with gusts reaching more than 300 kms per hour.

Most of the cyclones have winds blowing around 100 kms to 150 kms per hour. These do not cause much significant damage to crops, houses or the infrastructure. They are even beneficial at times as they bring with them water that is badly required to fill the reservoirs which provide for domestic, industrial and irrigation needs. Statistics tend to show that the island receives the visit of an intense and destructive cyclone with gusts of over 250 kms per hour about every 15 years.

A brief look at history

The Mascarene Islands (Mauritius, Réunion and Rodrigues) have remained havens of peace and quiet for very long. Arab traders were more interested in the Comoro Islands near the African coast or in Madagascar. Mauritius was however known as Dina Arobi in Arab naval charts of the tenth century. The island entered human history in the wake of the expeditions organised by the Portuguese to chart out the maritime route to India which would give them direct access to the precious spices and silk which so powerfully captivated the imagination of the Europeans.

Batholomew Diaz was the first European to penetrate the Indian Ocean after having rounded the Cape of Good Hope in 1488. Just above ten years later, in 1497, he was followed by his compatriot Vasco da Gama who travelled along the East African coast before heading for India. Another Portuguese captain, Fernando Pereira, "discovered" Mauritius in 1507 and gave it the name of his ship, *Cirné*. Still another Portuguese captain, Pedro Mascarenhas, has given his name to the Mascarene islands which, apart from Mauritius, includes Réunion situated at 200 kilometres to the southwest and Rodrigues situated at 600 kilometres to the east of Mauritius. The Portuguese were not very much interested in the Mascarene Islands, not even as a port of call. Their ships usually hugged the East African coast up to the port of Sofala in Mozambique before going straight to Goa on the western coast of India.

Soon however, the Indian Ocean was to witness a sharp competition among European powers for the supremacy of the maritime spice route and Mauritius was to play an important role in this adventure. The first to contest the Portuguese supremacy were the Dutch, followed by the French and the British.

The Dutch arrive ... with clumsy clogs !

The first Dutch sailors setting foot on the island at Old Grand Port in the Southeast on 17 September 1598 were struck by the beauty of the site. These sailors formed part of an expedition led by admirals Cornelius Van Nyck and Wybrandt Van Warwyck who gave the name of Mauritius to the island in honour of their Stathouder, Prince Mauritz Van Nassau.

The Dutch were immensely impressed by the island which offered a well protected harbour for their ships; pure cool water cascading from the mountains to revive the health of the sailors; fresh supplies of meat provided by large numbers of tame birds that could easily be caught by hand, by huge tortoises and by an abundant stock of fish in the lagoon. The first descriptions made by the Dutch sailors who landed at Old Grand Port express their feeling of wonder at the sheer abundance of natural riches that were exposed to their gaze.

" The sailors who had gone ashore came back in the evening bringing with them eight or nine big birds and a larger number of smaller ones that they had caught by hand. They had also found good fresh water coming down the mountain, so that this natural harbour is one of the best where one can put into port and the most convenient one for finding refreshments."

" On the 21st of September, they went to a different place … They captured a large number of birds which did not move away when they were approached, not even trying to fly … The land is mountainous, covered with green trees, most of which bear no fruits but among which the sailors found palm trees which provided an excellent meal to the fleet."

" The ground is covered with trees which grow so close to one another that it is difficult to go between them. The wood from these trees provides the best type of ebony in existence; it is black as tar and can be polished like ivory."

"The sea is so well stocked with fish that more than half a ton can be caught at one throw of the net. They also saw many tortoises, some of which were so large that four sailors could sit upon them …"

" The birds were so numerous, specially the turtledoves, that the sailors killed more than one hundred and fifty in the afternoon. Had they been able to carry more they would have killed as many as they wanted by hand or with a stick … "

Among these birds was to be found the *dodo*. This bird was as big as the swan. It had a large head covered with a hood-like skin. It had no wings but was covered with short feathers. It had no tail but sported four to five curly greyish feathers. The dodo had big tall feet. These sailors were also of the opinion that the eyes of the dodo were not very beautiful and that its flesh was unpalatable.

The Dutch transformed this enchanting site. The ebony forest was destroyed through intensive exploitation while the dodo for its part did not survive the passage of these first colonisers. It was already extinct by the seventeenth century.

The Dutch used Mauritius at first as a port of call for their ships heading towards the Far East. They then tried to establish a permanent colony on the island between 1638 and 1658 and again between 1664 and 1710. However, the colonisers were too few in number – never more than 400 including the garrison, the slaves and the rare women – and both these attempts failed. On abandoning the island for good in 1710, the Dutch left some deer, pigs and farm animals, a large number of rats and specially the sugar cane which was to play a major role in the future development of Mauritius.

The French are here to stay !

It was the arrival of the French which was to give the decisive impetus for the colonisation and development of Mauritius.

On the 20th September 1715, Captain Guillaume Dufresne d'Arsel arrived in Mauritius on board the **Chasseur**, and took possession of the island in the name of France and named it *Isle de France*.

A first contingent of sixteen settlers accompanied by a few slaves arrived in Port Nord-Ouest (the modern Port-Louis) on 24 December 1721, coming from the sister island of Réunion (then known as Isle Bourbon), occupied by the French since 1665. These "colons" faced a very difficult situation. They had to toil hard in the tropical heat in order to clear the land of its forests and bushes; to fight against the rats that threatened to destroy their crops and they had to overcome the damages caused by the cyclones. Discouraged, the first batch of colonisers left. But the French authorities had decided to keep their hold on Isle de France and new groups of settlers were sent, this time from France.

The situation was transformed with the arrival of Mahé de Labourdonnais as governor of the island in 1735. Endowed with a strategic vision, Mahé de Labourdonnais clearly saw the crucial role that Isle de France could play in the struggle for power between the French and the British in India and for the control of the Indian Ocean maritime trade route. He was bent upon converting the island into a solid power base for the extension of French influence in the region. Port-Louis became a full-fledged port and a shipyard capable not only of repairing but of constructing naval vessels. The town was fortified in order to resist any assault. The population increased rapidly and food production was encouraged both for local consumption and for the vessels calling at Port-Louis. The vision of Mahé de Labourdonnais was prophetic. Mauritius indeed played an important role in the numerous conflicts that opposed France against Great Britain during the eighteenth century in the Indian Ocean and in India : the War of the Austrian Succession (1740 -1748), the Seven Years War (1756 -1763), the War of American Independence (1778 – 1783) and the revolutionary and Napoleonic Wars (1793 – 1815).

In spite of the fact that the French won the naval battle at Old Grand Port on 23 August 1810, a British expeditionary force of 10,000 men coming from Rodrigues (which was conquered in 1809) landed on the north coast and overran the French defence forces composed of a maximum of 4,000 men, forcing the last French governor, General Charles Decaen, to capitulate on 3 December 1810.

The treaty of capitulation guaranteed that the properties, laws, customs and religions of the inhabitants would be respected. The terms of the Treaty were confirmed by the Treaty of Paris (1814) putting an end to the Napoleonic Wars. The British returned Bourbon Island to

France but kept Rodrigues and Isle de France which they renamed **Mauritius**.

The French colonisation was a total success and provided the basis for the future development of Mauritius. In 1809, the population was composed of 7,194 whites, 7,366 free and coloured and 58,728 slaves. The latter were "baptised and brought up into the Christian faith" as stipulated in the Code Noir which regulated the treatment of slaves in the French colonies.

During the period 1725 to 1810, Mauritius gradually changed its vocation. At first the island was utilised as a port of call for ships stopping over on their way to India. It soon grew into a commercial and maritime centre. Port-Louis conducted business extensively with British and French ports in India; with the ports on the East African coast and Madagascar; with those on the Arabic Peninsula as well as with the Dutch East Indies. In 1789 for instance, 203 vessels stopped at Port-Louis. This figure increased to 347 in 1803. Mauritius at that time amply deserved its motto " The Star and Key of the Indian Ocean ".

At the height of the struggle between the French and the British for supremacy in India and the Indian Ocean at the end of the eighteenth century, Mauritius became a centre from which pirates and corsairs such as Robert Surcouf, Lemême and others inflicted heavy damage to British trading vessels and contributed to the prosperity of the island. The nuisance value of Mauritius was such that the British decided to blockade the island as from 1809, to capture it in 1810, and to keep it under British rule, for Lord Pitt had stressed that the British would never become masters of India as long as the French controlled Isle de France.

At the end of the French colonial period, the island had also started to become a classical plantation colony. Slaves brought from Africa and Madagascar helped the French settlers produce the foodstuffs needed to satisfy the local population, the ships stopping over, the troops stationed on the island as well as those present during the periods of open conflict with the British.

Sugar cane had also started taking firm roots in Mauritius: its cultivation covered an area of more than 6,000 hectares in 1806.

Mauritius under British Rule : King Sugar

Sugar production was to dominate very rapidly the life, population and economy of the island under British rule. By 1860, there were more than 350 sugar factories in existence and the stone chimneys that still dot the Mauritian landscape amply show that sugar was the very lifeblood of the country.

The impetus for sugar production was provided by the British government's decision in 1825 to allow the importation of sugar from Mauritius on the same terms as sugar imported from the British West Indies. Sugar production nearly doubled between 1825 and 1826, increasing from 11,000 tons to 21,000 tons. Sugar exports to Britain escalated from 18,000 tons in 1827 to 51,000 tons in 1850 and 121,000 tons in 1860.

Another decision taken by the British was to have far-reaching consequences in Mauritius. Slavery was abolished in 1835 and after a 4-year compulsory apprenticeship period on their masters' plantations, the slaves became totally free. In 1839, these apprentices, numbering 53,000 deserted the plantations *en masse*. In 1840, only 4,000 accepted to continue working on their former masters' plantations while in the following year, not one of them accepted to renew their work contract.

The Mauritian planters were already aware since the 1820's that the days of slavery were numbered in Mauritius. They had therefore been urgently looking for an alternative labour source to maintain and extend their sugar cane plantations. In 1834, the first batch of Indian labourers came to Mauritius to work on contract on the sugar plantations. At first they came in a trickle. But the need for manpower was so pressing that the floodgates of indentured labour were soon opened wide.

From 10,000 yearly at the beginning of the 1850's, the flow of Indian immigrants reached 40,000 at the end of the decade. The large majority of these labourers came from the region of Bihar in northeastern India, embarking at the port of Calcutta. Other important batches embarked at the ports of Madras and Bombay. The wave of Indian immigration peaked during the 1860's, and started declining after the 1880's to stop completely during the second decade of the twentieth century.

The nineteenth century played a crucial role in the economic and human history of Mauritius. That was the period during which the island really became the melting pot of different races, languages, religions, traditions and cultures.

The freed slaves were converted to Christianity, while the Indian labourers brought with them part of the rich linguistic and religious heritage of their motherland. Hindi, Urdu, Tamil, Telegu and Marathi were languages that gradually took root in the island while Bhojpuri slowly became the lingua franca of the Indian community. Hakka and Cantonese were spoken by Chinese traders and shopkeepers. Creole, a new language born out of the meeting of French and the African languages during the French period, gradually established itself as the language of communication between the different groups in Mauritius: the French settlers, the British civil servants and administrators, the freed slaves, the Indian indentured labourers and the Chinese traders. Today Bhojpuri and Creole are firmly established as popular languages in Mauritius, while Creole has attained the status of national language as opposed to English which is the official language, and to French which is the language of the media and that of a big chunk of Mauritians. Mauritius is the only country in the world where French is progressing at the expense of English !

To this linguistic multiplicity must be added religious diversity. All the great religious traditions are represented in Mauritius: Christianity, Islam, Hinduism, Buddhism and Confucianism flourish side by side in harmony. Fifty-two per cent of the population are Hindus, 30% are Christians and 17% are Muslims.

Today 70% of the population descend from Indian immigrants, 26% are of African stock, while descendants of European and Chinese origins represent tiny minorities.

The different "communities" — a word which in the Mauritian context signifies religious or linguistic kinship — have lived side by side peacefully on the island, preserving their ancestral traditions. Since the last five decades, however, the relations between Mauritians of different communities have multiplied and strengthened under the pressure of economic, social and political evolution, leading towards the gradual standardisation of attitudes and behaviour. This unifying movement has been reinforced by the provision of free education at primary and secondary levels and by rapid industrialisation in the course of the last 20 years. These objective elements have given birth to a new complex Mauritian personality integrating ancestral traditions with the opening towards other values existing in a rapidly evolving plural society which is itself engulfed in the globalisation process submitted to the pressure of a dominant world culture.

Political life during British rule has been very dynamic. Relations between the sugar oligarchy and the British administration have often been conflictual, with the former bent upon defending its economic interests while the latter aimed at the peaceful development of the colony. They did not see eye to eye for instance on such issues as the abolition of slavery or the treatment meted out to the Indian indentured labourers, on the participation of the oligarchy in the administration of the country or on the issue of constitutional evolution. These matters were hotly debated in the press.

A Lively Press

Mauritius can boast of one of the most ancient traditions of freedom of the press, specially in the southern hemisphere. The first weekly was published in 1773 by Nicholas Lambert. It contained information which was useful to the colonial society of the time such as the arrivals of different vessels at Port-Louis, advertisements for the sale of slaves, cane plantations, immovable property, or social events.

The first daily, *Le Cernéen*, was launched in 1832 by the sugar oligarchy to campaign against the abolition of slavery. Since that time, innumerable dailies and weeklies, most of them shortlived, have been set up in order to discuss economic, social, political, literary and cultural matters in the different languages spoken in the island.

Enjoying total freedom of expression except for the laws on libel, these newspapers have played a crucial role in forging public opinion and in contributing to the social evolution of the country. There are today around twenty dailies and weeklies, mostly in French. They give expression to all shades of opinion and help bring to light the various problems affecting society. These can thus be discussed in the open before solutions are found in a spirit of consensus taking into consideration both the particular and the national interests. The press thus acts as a social regulator in this plural society and plays a decisive role in the formation of a spirit of tolerance and understanding required for the smooth evolution of the society. The press takes its role seriously and acts as a shield against any eventual sectarian or institutional drift.

Political Evolution

French plantation owners selected by the British governor formed part of the Council of Government as from 1825. Restricted franchise was introduced in 1886 for election to the Council of Government. This evolution was further accelerated in 1947 when franchise was widened to include all those who could read and write.

Meanwhile the trade union movement was born among the dockers and workers of the sugar industry. The Labour Party was set up in 1936 to continue the struggle started in the nineteenth century to improve the working and living conditions of plantation workers. It campaigned on a class basis for adult universal suffrage, internal political autonomy and for political independence. The struggle gathered momentum with the introduction of adult universal suffrage for the 1959 general elections. In spite of an attempt at dividing society along communal and religious lines, the sugar oligarchy failed to stop the country's march towards independence which was granted following the 1967 general elections. Independence was formally proclaimed on 12 March 1968 and the country is now a Republic since 1992.

The Constitution of Mauritius guarantees the right to property, and appeals against judgements of the Supreme Court are heard by the Privy Council in London. The Constitution also guarantees the exercise of all the freedoms prevalent

in democratic nations: freedom of speech, of expression, of movement, of religious belief... It also outlaws all forms of discrimination based on religion, race or sex. Observance of these essential clauses of the Constitution is enforced by the Supreme Court in the context of a parliamentary democracy where the separation of powers between the Executive, the Legislative and the Judicial branches of government is scrupulously respected and applied.

A brief survey of the economy

Up to the 1970's, the whole economy of the island rested on the production and export of sugar. Sugar produced by Mauritius was sold on the protected British market and 500,000 tons are now exported annually to the European Union at remunerative prices in the context of the Cotonou Agreement linking African, Caribbean and Pacific states (ACP) to the European Union (EU). The sugar industry has now embarked on a vast programme of modernisation and centralisation aimed at lowering its production costs in order to successfully face stiffer international competition. The industry has also started the production of value-added special sugars to satisfy foreign niche markets. Moreover, it is now engaged in an ambitious programme of energy production based on by-products of sugar, such as bagasse, with the total support of government. Apart from expanding into neighbouring countries, the sugar industry is also exporting its expertise to the African continent.

The sugar sector now represents less than 10% of the Gross National Product but it has kept its symbolic importance in the hearts of all Mauritians as the " mother industry ".

Since the 1970's, Mauritius has been transformed into a vast Export Processing Zone, employing more than 90,000 people in the textile and apparel sectors for export to the United States and Europe. Mauritian industrial units are specialising more and more in high value-added products while the manufacture of basic textile goods is being relocated to countries of the region such as Madagascar. The textile industry is also engaged in a vertical integration process in order to have easier access to the remunerative United States market.

Tourism is the third pillar of the Mauritian economy. Mauritius caters for an up-market tourism in its five-star beach resort hotels which are among the best in the world. Eco-tourism is also now gradually developing, allowing tourists to enjoy the beauty of the interior of the island, to interact with the local population and to discover the rich cultural diversity of this peaceful plural island society.

Since the last decade, the services sector has developed rapidly into the fourth pillar of the Mauritian economy. This segment encompasses the financial services, Offshore Banking and the Freeport. Double taxation avoidance treaties with numerous countries have accelerated the growth of this sector and helped to make of Mauritius the commercial hub of the Indian Ocean in continuance of a tradition established in the eighteenth century.

The rapid development of Information Technology and the determination of the authorities to transform Mauritius into a cyber-island are part of a strategy aimed at embarking the country upon a new phase of its development and deserving its new appellation of "Tiger of the Indian Ocean".

Port-Louis : The Heart of Mauritius

It is at the Company's Garden, in the very heart of modern Port-Louis, that the successful colonisation of Mauritius began with the arrival of a group of sixteen settlers accompanied by some slaves coming from neighbouring Bourbon Island on 24 December 1721.

Discouraged, however, by the magnitude of the task, these first settlers left one by one. They were replaced by others who came from Brittany in France aboard the *Diane* and the *Athalanta* on 5 April 1722.

In spite of the difficulties encountered to clear the land of its lush vegetation under the harsh tropical sun, in spite of the cyclones and the attacks by the fearsome armies of rats that had forced the Dutch to give up, these settlers courageously hanged on and their numbers increased gradually.

The arrival of Mahé de Labourdonnais as Governor of Bourbon Island and Isle de France on 4 June 1735 was going to have a profound influence on the destiny of Port Nord-Ouest – renamed Port-Louis – and on that of the new colony.

Mahé de Labourdonnais was the builder of Port-Louis. He initiated plans for the construction of the harbour and fortified the port so that it could withstand any enemy assault. The port was equipped not only to service ships but also to construct vessels for trade and war. Governor Mahé de Labourdonnais had a great ambition for Port-Louis : he wanted it to become an impregnable centre from which the French could control the maritime route to India and contribute effectively to the consolidation of French presence in India. It was in such a context that Mahé de Labourdonnais himself led a naval expedition from Port-Louis to blockade and obtain the capitulation of the British forces in Madras in 1746.

When Mahé de Labourdonnais was recalled to France in 1746, the colony had been established on firm foundations. There were 18,000 inhabitants (including 15,000 slaves) when he left as opposed to 3,000 when he arrived in 1735. Port-Louis had not only become the administrative capital of the French in the Indian Ocean, but it had also become an important trading centre and a cultural melting pot. Regular and fruitful commercial relations had been established with the ports on the East African coast, Madagascar, and India. Slaves had been brought from Madagascar and East Africa to work on the plantations, while others from India worked on the construction of ships, buildings and roads. The racial, linguistic and religious mix that characterised Isle de France right from the start was going to provide a distinct cosmopolitan flavour to Port-Louis.

The town has played an important role in the political history of Mauritius. During the French revolutionary period, the heart of the colony beat to the tune of events in Paris. The colonists participated actively in the process of change, and political power was exercised by their elected representatives in the Colonial Assembly. The settlers were quite prepared to adopt the motto "Liberty, Equality and Fraternity" of the new French Republic but they were not prepared to countenance the abolition of slavery as they considered that such a decision would spell ruin for themselves and for the colony. They therefore unceremoniously expelled the two representatives sent by the Paris Government to Isle de France in 1796 to ensure the implementation of the decree. The colony ruled itself in a state of semi-autonomy for some time until the arrival of a new governor, General Charles Decaen, who allowed the slave trade to continue.

Two strategic localities in Port-Louis have been the theatres of important events that have shaped the destiny of Mauritius: firstly, the *Champ de Mars* – a vast plain transformed into a racecourse by the British in 1812 – situated at the foot of one of the fortified hills, overlooking the town; secondly, the *Quay Square*, (integrated today in the Caudan Waterfront) facing the Government House built by Mahé de Labourdonnais. These two places have witnessed great popular meetings that have marked the struggle for justice and freedom since the 1940's.

Today, Port-Louis is the administrative, commercial and political capital of Mauritius. The modernisation of the harbour, the setting up of freeport facilities, the provision of business services such as offshore banking, have helped transform Port-Louis into the commercial hub of the Indian Ocean region and it now aims at becoming the commercial and economic bridge between Asia and Eastern and Southern Africa.

With its tourist shops, its cinemas and numerous restaurants providing a refined cosmopolitan cuisine, the new Port-Louis Waterfront – whose skyline draws its inspiration from local French colonial architecture – has become a popular leisure and promenade centre for the city population and for tourists alike. At a stone's throw is the central market, bubbling with life and colour, where exotic fruits, vegetables as well as local handicraft are sold in an atmosphere perfumed with the scent of those spices whose quest had incited traders as well as adventurers to leave the European shores and set sail for the East more than 500 years ago …

Let us go through some of the pictures of this multi-faceted, enchanting city …

Ile aux Fouquets with its lighthouse signals the entrance to Old Grand Port harbour
where the Dutch sailors first set foot on 17th September 1598.

Ile de la Passe, which directly commands the pass to Grand Port Harbour, has played
a crucial role in the naval battle won by the French over the British fleet in 1810.

Ile aux Aigrettes off Mahebourg, contains numerous endemic plants.

Aerial view of the village of Mahebourg, in the south of the island.

Right: Lion Mountain dominates the village of Old Grand Port which was the headquarters of the Dutch during the 17th century.

Port-Louis, the political, administrative and economic capital of the island, as well as its sole harbour.

The old and the new.
Left: new office buildings testify to the economic vitality of the city. Right: traditional stores face the new commercial centre of the Caudan Waterfront.

Sunset. Peace and quiet at the southern entrance of Port-Louis.
Right: The Caudan Waterfront mirrors itself in the harbour at night.

The Caudan Waterfront, with its colonial-inspired architecture, has become a tourist attraction at the heart of the city.

Port-Louis is also a destination for numerous cruises in the Indian Ocean.

Abundance and variety of goods at the Central Market.

———— Left: This picture captures the political, administrative and economic heart of Mauritius.Government House is situated at the end of the twin alley ————
of royal palm trees while the buildings on the right and left house the headquarters of the most important financial and commercial institutions.
In the foreground is the statue of Mahé de Labourdonnais, founder of Port-Louis, looking towards the Caudan Waterfront and the high seas.

Scenes of everyday life.

The Port-Louis museum in the shade of the centuries-old flamboyant trees.

The Champ de Mars racecourse, created by the British in 1812, is invaded by large crowds during the racing season.

The Trou aux Cerfs — a small extinct volcanic crater — dominates the town of Curepipe.
Both roads and towns serpent among the sugar cane fields.

Agriculture

The agricultural world is changing quite rapidly in order to adapt to the globalisation process.

The sugar industry is being restructured at both the levels of field work and industrial production of sugar. Rationalisation of human resources in field work is in progress, while the number of sugar factories will be reduced to achieve economies of scale and to cut production costs.

In order to obtain additional revenue, the sugar industry has also launched itself into the production of electricity from the by-products of sugar, such as bagasse. Energy is now being produced by a new process based on the use of coal and bagasse, thus reducing the country's dependence on imported petroleum products.

Village life which, until recently, was closely linked to agriculture, is rapidly changing. Gone are the days when whole families toiled in the fields producing sugar cane, tea, tobacco or vegetables and kept cows and goats for milk. The new generation of villagers, who are better educated and trained thanks to free secondary education provided since 1977, are deserting the fields and are eager to work in factories, in the resort hotels or in the services sector. Confronted with the resulting shortage of manpower, the agricultural sector is in the process of mechanising production techniques, and experimenting with biotechnology following research carried out by private and public sector institutions. The agricultural diversification programme of the third millennium will be based on the maximum utilisation of scientific techniques, and on the delocalisation of certain productions to the countries of the region on the model already experimented by the industrial sector.

The white curls of perfumed smoke rising gently from sugar factory chimneys, which testify to the immense work accomplished by descendants of settlers, slaves and indentured immigrants alike, to build a prosperous future for coming generations, might soon be an image of the past, fondly and nostalgically remembered by elder Mauritians.

Sugar cane cultivation has dominated the life of Mauritius for the last two centuries.
All the available plots of land were cleared and devoted to King Sugar.

Just before the harvest, the flowering sugar cane fields transform the countryside into a harmoniously undulating carpet.

"We must work to earn our bread" (Old Creole lullaby).
Right: Saltpans at Tamarin, on the western coast.

A variety of exotic fruits to suit all tastes …

Sugar consumed at source!

The interior highlands characterised by lakes, forests and green cane fields.

The Trois Mamelles Mountain (The Three Breasts) seen in the subdued evening light.

Spiritual Quest

The whole Mauritian landscape is impregnated with divine presence. A network of temples surrounds the sacred lake of Ganga Talao in the centre of the island; the monument dedicated to the Virgin Mary, Queen of Peace, visited by the Pope during his visit to Mauritius in 1989, overlooks the town of Port-Louis from the foot of Signal Mountain; pagodas and mosques are also situated at strategic locations far from the bustle of human activity. In all the big villages of the island, the visitor will recognise without any difficulty the characteristic Christian church, the Hindu temple or the Islamic mosque.

On the roadsides or at the foot of trees by the seaside, altars have been dedicated to gods and goddesses by the local population. The large variety of spiritual sites, whether big or small, elaborately built and decorated, or ascetic in their simplicity, are a symbol of the spiritual dimension of the Mauritian psyche.

The peaceful cohabitation of the great world religious traditions in Mauritius has given rise to a spirit of tolerance which has helped the country face its problems in an atmosphere of consensus integrating the aspirations of one and all.

Religious festivals are celebrated with great fervour by the different religious communities through such manifestations as pilgrimages, processions, ceremonies in churches or prayers at the family altar…

After having accomplished their religious rituals, Mauritians usually spend the rest of the day with their parents by the seaside, specially if a public holiday has been decreed for the occasion, which is quite often the case.

A village temple far from the bustle of day-to-day activities.

Venkateshwara Temple at the village of La Laura in the midst of lush greenery is an open invitation to meditation.

Exuberance of forms and colours characterise the delicately sculptured temples reminiscent of South India.

Pilgrims from all over the island converge towards the Ganga Talao,
considered as a sacred lake by the Hindus, on the occasion of the annual Maha Shivaratree festival in February/March.

Prayer and meditation.

Richly decorated temple at Trou Fanfaron, Port-Louis.

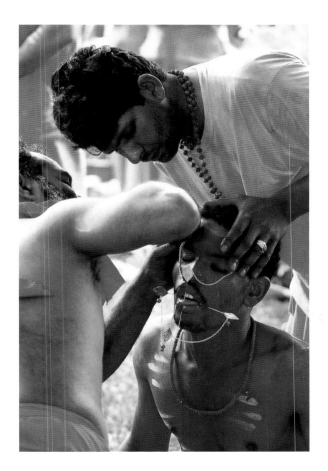

Devotees are ritually prepared for the Cavadee ceremony in honour of Lord Muruga.

Devotees have their tongues, cheeks, chests, forearms and legs
pierced with fine sharp needles for the Cavadee ceremony.

Prayer on the beach in honour of Goddess Doorga, one of the main Hindu divinities.

Immersion of the effigy of Goddess Doorga in the lagoon.

Christian presence: Ste-Anne Church at Chamarel village in the west on a Sunday morning.

Left: Pilgrims pay homage to blessed Father Jacques Désiré Laval who devoted his life to the evangelisation of freed slaves.
Right: Pamplemousses Church in the North.

The Islamic presence is visible everywhere on the island.
The Jummah Mosque – one of the most ancient of the capital – is a pure work of art.

Purification rites in the cool shade of the central courtyard …

Chinese traditions are perpetuated by young and old alike.

A richly decorated altar in one of the pagodas of the city.

Lights and Colours

The sixteenth century sailors waited impatiently for the stopover in Mauritius in order to restore themselves physically and mentally before continuing their journeys on the high seas. As in the days of old, Mauritius still offers the natural beauty of its contrasted landscape; the vivid brightness of its colours, the serenity of its daybreak and sunset; the pungent purity of its sea breeze brought by the trade winds; the caressing warmth of its crystalline waters in the protected lagoons.

Far from the hurly-burly, hustle and bustle of the megacities, let's take time to feel the soft touch of the fine white sand on the beach; to inhale the pure ocean air or to smell the sweet fragrance of a recently harvested sugar cane field; to discover the natural beauties of the island by foot or on bicycle; to chat with the hospitable, smiling, local population; or let's simply take time to sip a local punch lazily under the sun.

Yes, let's take a plunge to rejuvenate ourselves in this dream island. Accept our invitation to indulge…

The Coin de Mire at the extreme North.
Left: Pointe aux Canonniers in the North.

Flat Island with its sister-island, Ilot Gabriel.

Swimmer's paradise – warm crystalline waters of the lagoon with Ilot Gabriel in the distance.

Trou-aux-Biches beach.

Everyday life in fishing villages along the coast.

Land of rainbows …

The world famous Pamplemousses Botanical Gardens. Giant water lilies in the central pond.

Palm trees provide welcome shade in the midday heat.

Numerous species of palm trees are found in the gardens, many of them endemic to the Mascarene islands.

The talipot palm tree which flowers only once in its long lifetime.

Patchwork of colours on the slopes of Chamarel. Ile aux Bénitiers lies jewel-like in the lagoon while the Morne is on the far left.
Previous pages: the transparent lagoon of the Morne.

Total communion with the natural elements in the lagoon near Ile aux Bénitiers.

Generations have toiled patiently and with love to add a touch of beauty and colour to their environment.

The pink-red of the flamboyant tree integrates harmoniously into the green
of the sugar cane fields and the blue of the skies and waters of the coastal regions.

Mountains rising abruptly from the plains are relics of the volcanic past of the island.
Above: The Pieter Both; right: The Trois Mamelles and Rivière du Rempart Mountain.

Pink pigeons, green parrots, monkeys and the kestrel are the peaceful inhabitants of the mountainous highlands.
On the right: The Black River National Park.

Just not to forget that Mauritius is also part of Africa ! Deer farm in a savannah type landscape.

Metamorphosis of the countryside as a result of the ever-changing interplay of light, shade and colour …

The seven coloured earth dunes in the wilds of Chamarel. A unique phenomenon resulting from an original volcanic soil chemistry.

The quiet freshness of the Bassin des Aigrettes in the Black River National Park.

Two well-known aspects of Mauritian tourism: golf and water sports.
Right: The Morne peninsula afforded a refuge to slaves who fled their masters' plantations in search of freedom.

Man and the Sea. Fishing the tourist way or the local fisherman's way.

Simplicity of village life in an ever-changing decor …

Richness and diversity of marine life in the sparkling luminosity of the Mauritian atmosphere.
Left: The lagoon at Mahebourg. Right: Ile aux Cerfs.
Previous pages: The bungalows of Trou aux Biches Hotel scattered among the coconut trees, one of the jewels of Mauritian beach tourism.

Aerial view of part of the south coast near Blue Bay. Festival of different hues of blue.
Right: A few yards across, the blue lagoon has turned green!

All the beaches have character and personality but are not necessarily of fine white sand.

The tourist village resort of Grand Bay harmoniously blends the old and the new.

Regatta at the village resort of Mahebourg,
with the Mouchoir Rouge island (Red Handkerchief) as backdrop.

The sun drowning in its own flames!

Rodrigues

The rough nature of the Rodrigues countryside has chiselled a Rodriguan personality characterised by simplicity, straightforwardness, stoicism, solidarity and a spirit of proud independence. The Rodriguan population has retained the ancestral values of hospitality and greets all visitors with a large smile illuminating a face sculptured by time and the forces of Nature. The economy of the island was for long marked by self-sufficiency and autarky. The island is now slowly opening to the outer world as a result of the gradual development of tourism. The inhabitants, however, are determined to preserve their environment, their traditions and the rhythm of life that have made them unique in the Mascarenes.

Geography

Rodrigues is one of the Mascarene Islands. Situated 600 kms to the east of Mauritius, Rodrigues measures 8 kms from north to south and 17 kms from east to west. The island was born two and a half million years ago as a result of volcanic activity. Just like Mauritius, Rodrigues is also surrounded by a coral reef which has created a protected lagoon of 200 square kilometres.

The island is very mountainous. A hilly ridge crosses Rodrigues from the southeast to the northwest, from which a series of deep valleys descend to the narrow coastal plains. Mount Limon at 393 metres above sea level is the highest peak and is situated in the centre of the island. The hills have been subjected to natural erosion aggravated by the destruction of the indigenous forest. The temperature varies between 29°C and 33°C in summer (between November and April) and between 14°C and 18°C in winter (between May and October). As the other Mascarene Islands, Rodrigues is situated on the path of the tropical cyclones which crop up in the summer months. Mild cyclones passing near Rodrigues usually bring beneficial rain to this land often affected by drought.

Some historical notes

The island was discovered by the Portuguese navigator Diégo Rodriguez in 1528. Numerous attempts were made to colonise the island, of which the most well-known is the one conducted by François Leguat from 1691 to 1693, at the head of a small group of French protestants (Huguenots) who left Holland in search of a haven of peace where they would be free from the religious conflicts that were tearing Old Europe apart.

This attempt failed but in 1708, François Leguat published a description of his stay in Rodrigues providing precious information on the fauna and flora of the island on the eve of colonisation.

While Mauritius has witnessed the disappearance

of the *Dodo*, Rodrigues for its part has seen the disappearance of the *Solitaire*, a bird which could weigh up to forty-five pounds and whose flesh was "delicious" according to François Leguat and which – like the *Dodo* – could not fly as its " wings were too small to allow it to sustain the weight of its body ".

The Dutch, the French and the English tried to settle in Rodigues in the course of the seventeenth and eighteenth centuries. It is the French who succeeded in establishing a small colony in 1761. The island was captured by the British on 5 August 1809. The final attack on the French in Mauritius by the British was launched from Rodrigues in 1810. Rodrigues was to remain under British control and became a dependency of Mauritius before becoming part of the state of Mauritius on the accession of the country to independence in 1968. Rodrigues is represented in the National Assembly and it also enjoys a large degree of internal autonomy.

The population of Rodrigues numbers 35,000 of whom more than 95% are Roman Catholics.

Port Mathurin, in the north of the island, is the administrative capital of Rodrigues as well as its only port.

A brief glimpse of the economy

The economy of Rodrigues has almost exclusively been based upon agriculture, farming and fishing.

A third sector is slowly gathering strength : eco-tourism.

The Rodriguan population has lived in a state of quasi-autonomy for very long being given the difficulties in communicating with Mauritius. This is now a thing of the past as regular sea and air links have been established between the two islands. The arrival of the almost only ship plying between Mauritius and Rodrigues in the port of Port-Mathurin, is still a social event in Rodrigues as people from different parts of the island congregate at the harbour and exchange the latest news about Rodrigues and Mauritius. It is believed that there are today nearly as many Rodriguans in Mauritius as in Rodrigues itself.

Soil erosion and the chronic lack of water have hampered the development of agriculture. The main products are maize (for the local population and the farm animals), manioc (cassava), onion, garlic and citrus fruits, specially small limes, a speciality of Rodrigues which is pickled either alone or with tiny hot chillies ! These products, together with honey collected in the hills, are highly appreciated by visitors, just as the dried octopus which is found in the coastal villages and which is collected in the lagoons mainly by Rodriguan fisherwomen.

Cattle rearing is carried out mostly for local consumption. Families usually rear oxen, pigs, sheep and poultry which are left to wander free in nature.

Fishing is carried out by traditional methods in the lagoon which is now severely understocked. The number of fishermen exceeds 10,000 out of a population of 35,000.

Since the last few years, eco-tourism has started to take roots in Rodrigues, giving a new boost to agriculture, fishing and handicraft. The development of this new sector is being integrated into the overall harmonious development of the island so that the natural as well as the human environment is preserved. Rodriguan tourism aims at conviviality, based specially upon self-catering "gîtes", bed and breakfast guest houses, "table-d'hôte" meals; it generates interaction with the local population and stimulates the discovery of local products as well as the rich traditions and folklore of the population which include such elements as the "sega-tambour" from Africa and the lullabies from France. The most memorable ditty is the "romance zaricot", sung on the occasion of the sowing and harvesting of beans.

The impetus given to agriculture through the implementation of new projects, the diversification of the economy and the facilities granted for the setting up of small and medium enterprises, aim at creating gainful employment for the population on the Island of Rodrigues itself.

The sea has moulded the sturdy Rodriguan personality.

The rugged simplicity of Rodriguan landscape shaped by sea waves and trade winds.

A traditional home on the slopes of one of the numerous hills covering the centre of the island.

Port Sud-Est with Hermitage Island and Cat Island in the lagoon.

Channel at Port Sud-Est

The bungalows of Mourouk Ebony (left) and of the Cotton Bay Hotel (right)
hugging the few white sand beaches.

Houses clustering the hill dominating Port Mathurin, the capital.

The slow, dignified pace of life in the commercial centre of the town.

Saint Gabriel Church in the interior constructed as a self-help project.
The local population transported all the building materials on foot from Port Mathurin to the building site.

Fishing has for long been the lifeblood of Rodrigues.

Catches from the sea : octopus and mullet.
Right: The village of Port Sud-Est.

Limestone quarry … with fish being dried for dinner…

Trou d'Argent Beach.

Nature in all its splendour at Coco Island.